# Shy People Can Be Successful Too!

*How to achieve your dreams without changing your personality*

by
Adele de Caso

First Published in Great Britain In July, 2009 by Alenda Publishing.



ISBN 978-0-9561473-0-1

Printed by Graphics Services, Keele University, Staffordshire.

Bound by Book Binding Direct, Keele University, Staffordshire.

This book is dedicated to my wonderful family,
my husband Jaime and my children Sofia,
Phoebe and Javier.

# Contents

# Acknowledgements

My husband, Jaime de Caso for helping me with the title and for his constant support.

Paul MCgee (Author of SUMO - Shut Up, Move On) for his excellent advice.

John & Hazel Stephen for their inspiration, friendship and publishing advice.

Tom Walker for the design of the cover and illustrations.

Patricia de Caso for her proof-reading skills.

My children, Sofia, Phoebe and Javier. You give me the motivation to achieve so that I can spend time with you and help you to experience as many amazing things and places as possible.

Jan Ruhe who has inspired me in many ways through her books and seminars.

# Foreword

I wanted to write this book to share my experiences with those of you who think that because you are shy you can't get on in life and become successful.

This book isn't complicated. My objective was to create an easy to read book that could be carried around and pulled out whenever you have 10 minutes to spare.

You can be successful in whatever it is you want to do. All you need to do is develop a few skills and change a few habits. The best part is that you do not need to change your personality. You can be yourself!

I was a shy person with very little self confidence, but now I lead a very happy and fulfilled life and feel that I have achieved success in many areas. All sorts of people can create success in their lives.

In order to write this book, I have compiled over 10 years of notes that I have taken from various seminars, trainings, books and audios. I have carefully picked out the information that I feel has helped me the most and that will be most relevant to you. I passionately want to share this information with you. It has made such an immense difference to my life and I believe it can do the same for you.

Throughout this book, I will introduce you to the key things that I have learned that have helped me tremendously. If you apply them in your own life they can make a positive difference to you too.

By applying what I am going to share with you in this book, I have been able to achieve things that I never thought were possible. I have twice presented on stage to 5,000 people, travelled around the world, invested in property, run a business that turns over in excess of 1 million pounds per year, developed lots more confidence, moved to a 5 bedroomed detatched home, bought a villa and an apartment in Spain and at the same time raised a wonderful family. The things that I have achieved may not necessarily appeal to you, but you can apply the principles to achieve whatever it is that **you** want.

All the things that I will be covering in this book have helped me, but it is important that you just take from it what you feel will help you and leave the rest.

There is no question that shyness can deprive us of embracing opportunities and doing things that other people take for granted. But why should it? What if we didn't give in to our shyness and instead chased our dreams and set out to achieve our goals? What if?

Shyness can sometimes really challenge us and it can make our lives quite difficult. It can stop us from pursuing our dreams and ambitions. However, it doesn't have to be this way. There are lots of successful people who have struggled with shyness at some point in their lives, but they didn't let it stop them. They include:

Thomas Edison, inventor of the light bulb.

Albert Einstein, world famous scientist.

Tom Hanks, a very successful actor.

Michelle Pfeiffer, a very successful actress and hands-on mum.

It's hard to believe that these successful people have had challenges with shyness. The fact that they have, proves that shyness doesn't have to stop you from achieving your dreams.

You are certainly not alone if you are shy. I was quite surprised to learn from statistics that between 40 and 45 percent of all people consider themselves to be shy. Now you will probably feel lots better already, knowing that you are not in a minority.

If you can learn to control your shyness and not let it control you, you can be a success. You don't have to change who you are, just the way you think.

# Success-what does it mean to you?

It doesn't matter what sort of person you are, you can be successful. If you are a shy person, you do not have to become an extrovert to be successful.

Everyone's definition of success is different!

You might simply want to be a brilliant mum, dad, husband or wife. Some of you may wish to become very successful in your chosen career. To some people, success is starting up and growing a hugely successful company, to others it is to be financially free. This could mean having enough money to enjoy all the luxuries that life offers, like travelling the world, staying in top class hotels, living in your dream house and driving your dream car.

You need to come up with your own definition of what success means to you.

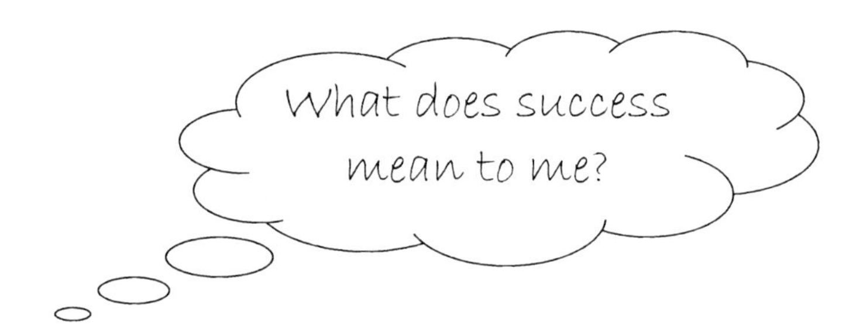


What is it that would give you tremendous joy and satisfaction in your life?

Don't limit yourself; you can be whatever you want to be. The world is your oyster.

The aim of this book is to help you on your way to becoming a success in whatever area you choose, regardless of your character.

# My Story

Growing up, I was a really shy, self conscious person with no self confidence. I used to hate it when people said I was 'quiet'. It just made things worse. I was even less likely to say anything then because attention had been drawn to me!

At school I was the one who sat at the back, never spoke up in class, and at college and university I was much the same.

My first job after leaving university was in a laboratory at the local hospital. At first it was okay, but I soon became very unhappy. I returned home in tears on numerous occasions, because the more I tried to do everything right, the more I seemed to get things wrong. The more I got things wrong, the less confident I became.

I didn't look forward to going to work in the mornings. I hardly ever got to work early, but if I did I would sit in the car until the very last minute before entering the building. I used to spend the lunch hours looking in the job centre for alternative employment! I felt that my lack of self-confidence was ruining everything. I knew I was capable of doing a good job, but I was so scared of making mistakes, I couldn't relax.

I attended an assertiveness course whilst working at the hospital, only to find that everyone on it (except my friend who I had gone along with) seemed to have been born an extrovert! I was far from happy.

One day, I was invited by a friend of mine to a business meeting in a hotel. It was a little secretive, but I had a lot of respect for my friend who was a school teacher by day. She said that she and her partner were picking up lots of money, every week from a simple business. To say I was excited was an understatement; this could have been the escape route that I was looking for!

My husband Jaime, and I, arrived at the meeting and were introduced to a few people before being directed to where the presentation was to take place. It wasn't long before we realised that we were not going to become rich overnight. For a start we hadn't got £3,000 to spare for the fee to get started, and secondly this business could never last, there wasn't even a product or service! To say the least, we left the meeting feeling gutted. Our hopes had been dashed within 20 minutes of sitting down!

Life carried on as normal for a while, but it was not many weeks later when I received a phone call at work from an excited Jaime, informing me that he had found our route to wealth. I thought to myself, 'Oh no, not another one of those dodgy schemes again!'

That night I found myself watching a company video for a home-based business opportunity with a British Plc. I had never come across the form of business that was being presented to me before, but it looked really exciting. There were people on the video from all walks of life and they were earning some incredible incomes, and on a part time basis. We thought it had to be worth a closer look. The next evening, after a chat with the person who had recommended the business to us, we signed on the dotted line and were the proud owners of our new home-based business. This is where it all started.

In this book I am going to share with you the opportunities that were presented to me and the information I accessed whilst building our business. It introduced me to a whole new world and I discovered that I could become everything and anything I wanted to be regardless of my shyness.

I want you to believe that you too can become a successful person because if you believe you can, you can. If I can change my life for the better so can you!

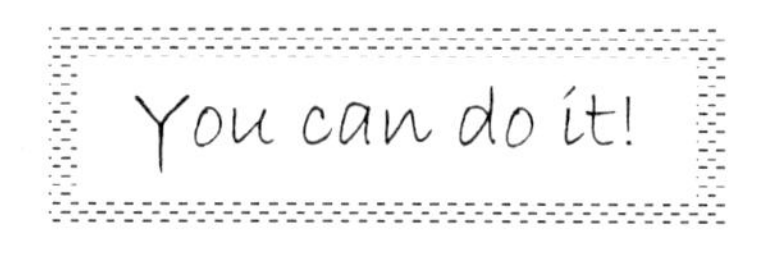


I am now sitting writing this book on the balcony of our Spanish penthouse. We are not just on holiday here; we are living here for 10 months! I am looking at the mountains and the sea. It is November and I am wearing shorts and a T-shirt!

Having dropped off our two daughters at their Spanish school this morning, I went to do some shopping in our local town but before doing so, stopped off at one of our favourite coffee shops for breakfast, did a bit of reading and enjoyed a spot of 'people watching'. I then moved on to browse the local market and one of my favourite fashion stores. After this, I made my way to my Spanish lesson. Jaime and I wanted our children to be bi-lingual from an early age, so we decided to enrol them in a totally Spanish school. Jaime is half Spanish so it made sense for all of us to study the language, hence the Spanish lessons!

10 years ago I would not have believed this lifestyle to be possible, but here I am. I have to keep pinching myself!

# Chapter 1 - Reading and learning can change your life

Reading has changed my life. Fact! I had never picked up a book since leaving university. To be honest, the text books I studied during my degree course were enough to put many people off for life!

I read the odd fictional book when I was on holiday but that was about it...... until I was introduced to personal development and self improvement! There are so many books available on a variety of different topics. I suppose I just never realised that these sort of books existed. A colleague loaned me a couple of books to start with, and a set of motivational audios. This set of audios was to be the turning point in my life. Whenever I got into the car, I would put in the tapes. My car was like a new kind of university! The difference was, I was so eager to learn more and more, I never wanted to stop listening, unlike in my lectures where I often found myself clock watching!

*My mini university!*

I started to read one book after another and couldn't believe how much better I started to feel. The reading gave me a whole new outlook on life, I realised that I didn't have to be shy little me; I could become something more, whatever I wanted to be.

I found out about more and more books that successful people were reading. It made sense to me that the books that they were reading were the ones that I should be reading. If they had read it, I wanted to read it!

Lots of people have had their lives changed by reading one book in particular. I feel that I have been influenced by many books but one that does stand out amongst the rest is The One Minute Millionaire by Mark Victor Hanson and James Allen. This book inspired me to write my own book and gave me the confidence and the belief that I had something to share that would help many people out there who suffered with their shyness like I once did.

## Tips on reading

You don't need to read for hours and hours every day, anything from 15 to 30 minutes is better than nothing. Reading for this amount of time every day is a great way to start making a positive change in your life, and if you practise this for long enough it becomes a habit. It is very easy to do, but you have to be careful because it is also very easy not to do! Reading for 15 minutes is only

1 percent of your day. It is a tiny investment of your time, but it can reward you massively.

## Routine

It helps if you can get into some sort of routine when you first start reading. You can read just before you go to bed at night, first thing in the morning, or whatever is easiest for you to maintain.

## Pockets of time

I find that keeping a book in my handbag is great for those occasions when you feel like you are wasting time in queues or waiting rooms for example. If you have a book with you, you can just take it out and read while you are waiting. This gives you a whole new outlook on queuing! I used to get really fed up if I had to queue; now I see it as an excellent opportunity.

When I was working, part of my job involved seeing patients on an appointment basis. I used to take my book with me to work because if ever there was a gap between the patients I could read for a few minutes.

## Audio

Most books are available today as audios too. You can either purchase them on CD or download them from the internet for your MP3 player. You can listen to the audios whilst you are driving, walking, jogging or even doing the housework! This method is really useful if you are particularly short on time or if you don't really like reading books that much.

## Reading technique

Believe it or not there is a special way to read a book so that you get the most out of it.

- Read the covers first and then skim through the rest to get the point of the book.

- Then read through the whole book, and highlight certain sentences that stand out to you. You can also write in the margins if you like. (This did not come easily to me to start with. It felt wrong to scribble in books!)

- You should then come back to your book a few weeks later and review paying particular attention to the bits you have highlighted.

When I started to read in this way, I got so much more from each book that I read. I found that making notes and highlighting throughout the book was especially helpful because I could always go straight to my favourite or most important bits without having to re-read the whole book.

Of course, the secret is to act on the knowledge that you have gained from reading and put the ideas that you have learned into practice. It's no use having the knowledge if you are not going to use it!

At the back of this book, there is a list of my favourite titles. Every single one of these has inspired me, motivated me or educated me in some way and I wouldn't be without them now. I recommend that you read or listen to as many of them as you can and take from them what is relevant to you.

Always look for opportunities to better yourself. If you are not a member of the library, then become one as soon as you can. The books are free! Access this free information. It amazes me that only a very small percentage of the population own a library card.

I am also amazed that the majority of books that I have on my bookshelf cost me less than £10! The information on these pages is potentially life-changing and it costs less than going to the cinema for two!

Attend courses and seminars and learn all you can, soak up the information like a sponge.

We can choose to learn or we can choose not to. You have already taken the first step. If this is your first personal development book then congratulations! I hope I inspire you and it becomes the first of many.

# Chapter 2 - Simple communication skills

One of the best things I have learned over the past 10 years is how to use a few simple communication skills.

When you are shy, it is often hard to either get a conversation going or to maintain a conversation. I began to feel more and more confident in talking to people, just by utilising some of the simple techniques that I will share with you now.

## Listening

A very important part of communication is the art of listening. We have two ears and one mouth for a good reason!

When you are shy you might find, like I did, that whilst the other person is talking, you are so busy worrying about what you are going to say when it's your turn to speak, that you haven't really listened at all to what the other person has said. Try to relax and don't worry too much about what you are going to say when it's your turn. You will find that the conversation will flow naturally because you have genuinely listened to what the person has said.

## Ask questions

Asking people questions and being genuinely interested in the answers makes them feel important. It is also a great way of getting a conversation going. The best questions to use are open-ended questions because they will give you more than a 'yes' or 'no' answer and get the person talking. Closed questions can be answered with a 'yes' or a 'no' so are not the best conversation starters.

Example of an open-ended question:

*"What are you doing at the weekend?"*

Example of a closed question:

*"Are you working tomorrow?"*

When you show an interest in people by asking questions, people will think **you** are really interesting! You don't have to constantly think of interesting things to say, you just have to ask more questions. People are more interested in themselves than in anyone else, and if you show a genuine interest in them, they will think very highly of you.

## Use people's names

It is very important that you use a person's name whenever you can. This makes them feel special and is another way of showing that you are interested in them.

A lot of people have difficulty remembering names. It is quite common for someone's name to have been forgotton just 5 seconds after being introduced. This is down to distractions such as thinking about what to say next or taking in other things about the person. It can also be down to you thinking about how you are coming across to that person. When you are introduced and told the person's name, you could say:

"Nice to meet you.....*(their name)*".

If you then repeat their name several times to yourself and use it in the conversation whenever you can, you will have a much higher chance of remembering it.

Never apologise for being terrible at remembering names. When you say this you are obviously going to be terrible at it. You have just told yourself that you are! It doesn't give the other person a great impression either.

## Akward silences

Regardless of what you might think, it is acceptable to have silences during conversations. It gives each person chance to think about what is being said. Try to become comfortable with 'uncomfortable' silences if that makes sense!

## You are interesting!

Sometimes shy and quiet people think that they are boring and that no-one will be interested in what they have to say. This is not true and is merely in the imagination. I have already mentioned that asking questions is a great way of appearing interesting. When you try this out, you will probably find that you have things in common with people that you didn't realise you had. Once you discover common interests, it will become a lot easier to talk to these people. Don't avoid conversations because you think you are boring. This will only lower your confidence and also send out the message to others that you are lacking in confidence too.

## Smile

Smiling is very important. If you smile you come across as a warm and friendly person and people will want to be around you. People who receive your smile will see it as a compliment and it will usually make them feel really good. By smiling, you are also saying that you are open to starting a conversation. You can have some fun with smiling. For example - see how many people you can give your smile to in a day! It is an amazing feeling when you see someones face change just because you have smiled at them.

## Body language

Body language research has shown that over 70 percent of communication is non-verbal.

If your body language is closed, it can cut short your conversations. Signals which indicate that your body language is closed can be lack of eye contact, no smile and closed posture.

First impressions are important when you are communicating with someone for the first time, so it is worth making sure that your body language is open. Your posture tells people whether you are open for conversation or not. Try to avoid folding your arms or crossing your legs and also don't cover your mouth or touch your face. This can indicate that you are deep in thought and are not to be interrupted. If you lean forward slightly when someone is talking to you, you indicate that you are interested in them and what they have to say and it encourages them to continue talking.

Offer your handshake when you are introduced to people or meet people for the first time. I think it is very important to have a firm handshake too. Smile at the same time and you will come across as a friendly, approachable person.

## Eye contact

It is important to maintain eye contact. Looking someone in the eye when you are having a conversation with them is another sign that you are genuinely interested in what they are saying. It is fine to have some breaks from the eye contact and look at other parts of the person's face, as long as you return to eye contact every now and again. If you feel awkward maintaining eye contact, just try it for a short time to begin with and then gradually increase the length of time until you feel more comfortable. Be careful not to go over the top with eye contact though. If you stare at someone it can make them feel quite uncomfortable, so try to keep it natural and relaxed. Nodding your head is another indication that you are listening well. You can couple this with a smile too.

When you are looking for people to start a conversation with, keep your eyes open for people who have friendly faces and open body language. You can then go up to them and start a conversation. A good way to get started is to use a compliment.

Shy people will not often start conversations because they are worried that the other person will not be receptive towards them. Choose people who look more receptive and you will increase the chance that the person will want to talk to you. Look for smily, friendly faces and open body language. Most of the time people will respond to you in a positive way and even if they don't, what have you lost?

Just a few more things you should think about when holding a conversation with someone. Try to avoid repeating what the other person has said, interrupting mid sentence and finsishing people's sentences off for them! Let the person speak, pause and then answer them.

## Just to recap:

- Listen to what the person is saying.
- Ask questions.
- Always smile.
- Use people's names.
- Be interested in people.
- Make people feel important.
- Be aware of your body language.

Now with these simple skills, you can get out there and start practicing. Remember that you will naturally find some people easier to talk to than others. Try to practice talking to a wide range of people, starting with the people who you find most approachable, and before long you will be amazed at the results!

# Chapter 3 - Building your confidence

How often have you wondered how different life would be if you oozed confidence?

*"If only I had confidence I would.......... ".* Sound familiar?

Confidence is something that develops over a period of time. I found that confidence began to appear as I started to believe in myself. The more you believe in yourself, the more confident you will become.

# Believe in yourself

## How to start believing in yourself

A lack of confidence often stems from a feeling of insecurity, so a good start is to try and think of just a couple of things that you like about yourself. These could be physical attributes or personal qualities, whatever you like:

- Recognise your strengths.
- Know that you have some special qualities.
- Acknowledge your small achievements.
- Don't worry what other people think.

Being self confident doesn't mean you are an extrovert. Many self confident people are quiet individuals; they simply have a higher level of self esteem.

A great way of developing your self confidence is to do something that you love, either as a hobby or a profession. When you immerse yourself into something which you are really excited about, you naturally develop confidence. This is because people are very often good at the things that interest them the most. When you are constantly enjoying what you are doing, you will not even think about what other people are thinking of you.

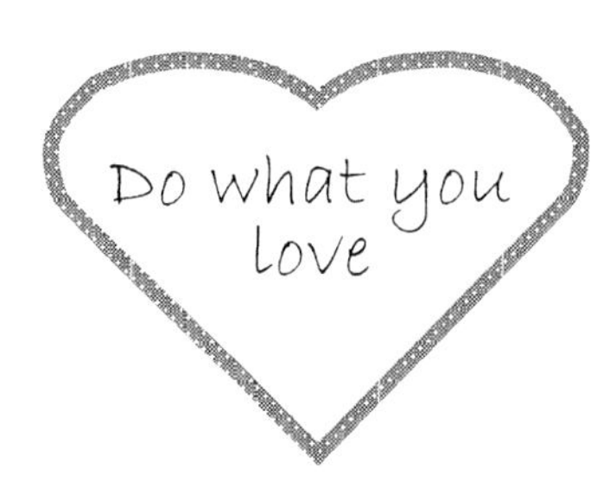


## Dress for success

By dressing for success, I don't necessarily mean suiting up every day; I just think it is important that you feel good about how you look and that you are smart and presentable. How you feel about how you look makes a difference to how you act. If you don't feel right you will not perform to your full potential, because you will be too busy worrying about your appearance. Get organised with your wardrobe and make sure that you have at least a couple of outfits that you feel really good in. Invest in a couple of good items if you need to. Or, you could just purchase a few accessories to add some interest to your existing clothes. Plan your outfit the night before so that you don't waste time in the morning trying to pick out something to wear. If you are rushing around trying to get the children ready for school etc. you will just throw on the first thing that you come across and you may not feel right because you will feel like you have not made an effort.

Just a few minutes spent the night before can save a lot of time, stress and make a huge difference to how you feel.

## Dealing with particular events

Sometimes particular events or situations can seem to enhance your shyness. For example, walking into parties where there are large groups of people, or being present in a meeting where you have to speak up in front of a room full of people. Before I learned to control my fear of these situations, each time I spoke up in front of two people or more, my chest would turn from pale white to a bright red blotchy mess within seconds of opening my mouth, and I could feel myself getting hotter and hotter the more attention people paid to me. If you can relate to this, while you are learning how to deal with the situation, just wear something that covers the chest area so that at least if the colour change is occurring, only you will know about it!

The communication skills that I talked about in the previous chapter are a great help for talking to people at parties etc. so just practice using them until you feel more relaxed.

You will find that when you start asking people questions and finding out about them and their lives, you will completely forget about yourself and become genuinely interested in the other person.

If you work, chances are you may have to attend meetings from time to time. A great tip for those of you who are not comfortable with this is to arrive a little early, maybe 10-15 minutes, simply so that you can engage in small talk and make yourself familiar with people before the meeting starts. This gives you time to warm up and adjust to the environment. Most shy people will actually do exactly the opposite; they will turn up late so that they can slip into the meeting at the last minute and not have to engage in small talk. This is what I used to do when I arrived at work in the morning. I would sit in my car on the carpark until the very last minute and only enter the building when I absolutely had to.

If you don't relish the thought of speaking up in meetings or other situations which may require you to do so, remember that you are not on your own with your shyness. Chances are that half of the other people in the room are in the same position as you.

## Comfort zone

Another way of building your confidence and personally developing yourself is to do things, small things at first, which take you out of your comfort zone. We all get comfortable at one time or another. You can even get comfortable with being shy. I suppose you just get used to living with it and any form of change can seem like too much of an effort. It is important to recognise this when it happens if you want to achieve success in your life, because for any form of improvement to occur, change is required and this inevitably means stepping outside of your comfort zone.

Things that make you slightly uncomfortable are the ones to start with. It could be anything. For example you could introduce yourself to someone on the school playground who you haven't spoken to before, or you could start up a conversation when you are in the checkout queue at the supermarket or in the lift at work. A great thing that you can do is to pay someone a compliment because you know that 99 percent of the time the response will be a positive one. Not only will you feel good because you have stepped out of your comfort zone, but you will have made someone else's day too!

Accepting compliments is equally as important. When someone pays you a compliment it is so easy to just brush it off. How often has someone complemented you on an outfit or an item of clothing for example and you respond with something like "Oh this old thing" or "Oh it's just something I threw on"? Many of us have. It is hard at first but try really hard to accept the compliment, afterall it is actually impolite not to. All you have to say is “thank you”. It's as simple as that!

If you find that you always feel uncomfortable at social functions or in situations where you will be amongst other people, a tip for you is to think ahead of things that you can say to the strangers you meet there. Have something to say, maybe read the newspaper or a magazine to get the current talking points of the day.

So, by simply paying a few compliments or starting some brief conversations, you can gradually start to expand your comfort zone. It may seem difficult at first but you will soon get used to it and you will get tremendous satisfaction when you do this and feel a real sense of achievement too.

## How I went from shy, insecure little me to giving a presentation to 5000 people!

Obviously, a series of smaller steps led me to this achievement but the point is I made it because I developed confidence in myself, something which I thought was impossible at the start.

I remember how I used to dread giving talks in lessons at school and how I even hated putting my hand up in class for that matter. Public speaking was always something that I would go to great lengths to avoid, until I started my business that is. I started off presenting 5 minute slots at our business open evenings. This I hated at first. The first time, I was talked into it with very little notice but I think it did me the world of good because I certainly would not have volunteered myself. This was the starting point and I just kept doing it, my slots got a little longer and I progressed on to training sessions. I couldn't have done this however if it wasn't for the personal development that I had come across, in the form of the books, the audios and the mentorship from successful people. I gradually gained belief in myself and began to enjoy speaking, it felt good because I was sharing information with people and showing people how they could start to change their lives like me.

A few years later I was asked to share my story at a bigger event, there would be about 400 people there. I agreed to it although I knew it was going to be a real challenge. This is an approach I always take, even if I don't know how I am going to pull it off. Once you are commited, somehow the steps seem to unfold in front of you. The talk went really well. Don't get me wrong, it was totally nerve racking, but I got through it, and it gave me a tremendous amount of satisfaction.

When I was asked to speak at the National Indoor Arena, Birmingham, in front of 5000 people, I couldn't believe it at first, but again I said yes straight away and knew that I would do whatever it took to get it right. This had been a secret dream of mine for a long time. I had seen many people share their story on that stage and always found it so inspirational. I had also taken many notes from the amazing speakers who had stood there and showed everyone how to succeed. And now, people were going to be taking notes from me! How amazing was that?

It went well once again, although parts of it are still a little blurred to say the least! I have since been up there again and have to say it is one of the best experiences I have ever had.

So, you can set your mind to achieving anything you want to. If something seems too huge a task, just break it down into a series of smaller, manageable steps and accomplish one at a time. The same idea applies to writing this book. One word at a time, one paragraph at a time, one page at a time, one chapter at a time, until it is finished!

# Chapter 4 - What do you really want?

I strongly believe that everyone should follow their dreams. It all starts with goal setting which is simply writing down your dreams and ambitions and putting a date on them. Decide what you want and write it down. It couldn't be easier. Anyone can do it.

Shy people should not be afraid of goal setting. I actually found that it was a way of escaping into my own little world where I could dream to my heart's content. I always had big dreams when I was younger but they had since faded into the distance. When I was first introduced to goal setting and realised that I could revive and achieve those dreams, I became very excited!

I was very fortunate to come across the concept of goal setting. Most people don't know what it is, and even if they do, they find it hard to understand the concept. Of those people who do understand the concept, still very few will take the time to write their goals down, and this I find quite hard to understand.

I think it is likely that people find it hard to write down what they really want because they are afraid that if they write it down and then they don't achieve it, that they will feel like they have failed. The way I look at it is, you have failed anyway if you don't write them down in the first place. When you put pen to paper something magical happens. It's as though you have just committed to truly wanting those things to become reality.

You should always write out your goals in the present tense as if you have already achieved them. This way they will be more powerful. My goals are written down in lots of different places. To start with, when I first discovered goal setting, they were simply written down on an A4 sheet of paper. I then progressed to writing them in a hard backed journal so that I knew I would never lose them. I also keep a small goal book for jotting things down whenever I think of something I want. It is just a little note book that is small enough to fit in my handbag in case anything comes to mind while I am out and about.

I also have lists pinned up on the wall where I know I will see my goals every day. At the moment there is one on the wardrobe door so that I see it first thing every morning. You can have a list anywhere you like, on the fridge door, the bathroom door or in your car for example.

Something which I have used more recently which has had amazing results is keeping my goals on little cards in my purse. Each one is written out on a 2 x 1 inch card and they are in a position where every time I go into my purse when I am shopping, I see them and quickly flick through them. If your goals are with you as you go about your daily business, they are always going to be at the forefront of your mind.

Another great way of goal setting is to make a goal board. It is simply a pin board or similar to which you can pin pictures and photographs of things that you want. My goal board lives over the office desk. Some people prefer to decorate their fridge with their goals! Just do whatever works best for you.

I have also more recently put together a picture goal book. For this I have used a photo album. At the top of each page my goal is written out and underneath the page is filled with pictures of the goal and everthing that comes with its accomplishment.

So, as I said previously, most people never make a list of their goals during their lifetime. If you decide to write your goals down having read this chapter, you will put yourself into an exclusive group of people.

Only 3 percent of the population write their goals down on paper. This 3 percent include some of the world's most successful people. Do you think that knowing that you belonged to such an exclusive group would go a long way to making you feel at least a little bit more confident? I certainly do. I can assure you that it had a massive effect on me!

When I look back to the time when someone advised me to write out my goals for the first time, I can remember doubting the fact that it would work, but at the same time, didn't really think I had anything to lose, so I did it anyway. As I said before, I was excited to think I could revive my dreams. How glad I am that I did!

Recently, I took out the first list of goals I ever wrote. This was 12 years ago. Amazingly, running through the list, I could tick off more or less everything that was on there! At the time of writing the list, I had included things that seemed a little bit far fetched, but they have now been accomplished. Don't limit yourself to what seems realistic. If you want it, write it down!

Goal setting should be fun, never a chore. One of the things I love to do is look at show homes when a new housing development appears. Jaime and I have looked at lots of show homes as purely goal setting exercises! When we first started to do this, quite often when we went into really large houses, the sales person would look at us in disbelief because we were young. I remember going into a house one day and when we asked how much it was, we were told that it was "Very expensive"!

On another occasion, I entered a sales office and was asked if I was looking for my parents! I suppose they were just not used to people in their early twenties looking at houses that were worth so much, but it did start to annoy me slightly! Afterall, for all they knew, we could have won the lottery!

We were determined that this wouldn't happen again, so the next time we had a show home to look at, first of all we did a spot of goal setting involving Jaime's favourite, cars! We went along to the local BMW dealer and managed to arrange a test drive of the 3 series cabriolet. It was gorgeous! We had it for the best part of the day, so there was plenty of time to drive up to the mansions we had planned to view. As we arrived in the soft- top, we pushed the button to trigger the hood to electronically close, making sure we could be seen from the sales office. As you can probably imagine, the staff bent over backwards to help us!

Make goal setting fun

Once you have written out your goals, they can be altered. You may want to amend the dates or you may just decide that there is something on the list that doesn't really motivate you anymore. This is absolutely fine. There is no point having something on your list that you are not passionate about, because it will not drive you. Goals are like magnets pulling you in the right direction

Goals can be short term, medium term or long term. I class short term goals as anything up to a year, medium term goals from 1 year to 5 years and long term goals from 5 years to 10 years. It is important to have a good mix of short, medium and long term goals. When you write down your long term goals they may seem miles away, so, this is why we should have plenty of short and medium term goals to act as stepping stones along the way.

Goals should be measurable too. For example, if you want to earn extra money, state how much, and by what date you want to be earning it.

An example of a measurable goal is:

"I earn £100,000 per year" *Date ????.*

What I recommend that you do now is to stop reading at the end of this chapter and write out your list of goals. There is a special section at the back of this book where you can write your first list. Have a 'brain storming' session and jot down everything that comes into your head. Let your imagination run wild, there are no restrictions. You can add the detail and dates later. This initial excerise simply gets your thoughts down on paper.

Remember, you will be joining that top 3 percent of people just by doing this. You will be on your way to success!

# Chapter 5 - Make it happen

This chapter covers some techniques and theories that you can take advantage of to help you to move more rapidly towards your goals.

## Visualisation

I have had a lot of success with a technique called visualisation. I found it an extremely interesting subject the moment I started to read about it. However it wasn't easy at first to get into the habit of using the technique, although it did soon become much easier as I started to establish some sort of routine.

Visualisation involves seeing the things that you want in your mind. You can visualise material things or personal qualities that you want to acquire. You could visualise a more confident you! For example, I would visualise myself walking into a room, being greeted by everyone in there and I would feel self confident and relaxed. If I had a public speaking event coming up, I would picture the whole thing in my mind first. I would see myself delivering an excellent presentation and then everyone would clap and cheer. Some people would even stand up. After the presentation, people would approach me and tell me how they enjoyed it and how I had made a difference.

A few years ago I set a goal to own a mini cabriolet, my all time favourite car. Here's how I would visualise owning the car. If it was a warm, sunny day, I would pick up my oldest daughter from school and on the way home we would open all the windows, put the music on and drive home with the wind blowing through our hair, imagining that we were in the mini with the roof down. I would even imagine I was holding the chunky, leather steering wheel as I drove. It really worked, I really felt like I was driving my dream car, then 6 months later, I was!

At this point, I suggest that you choose something that you would like to have, somewhere you would like to go or something you would like to do and then, go and investigate it. If it is a holiday for example, go to the travel agent and get the brochures. Sit down with the agent and plan your dream vacation. If it is a car, go and test-drive it, if it is a house arrange a viewing. Whatever it is, go and create the feeling of what it would be like to be achieving it by giving yourself a taste of your dream.

## The Law of Attraction

When I first discovered and started to read about the Law of Attraction, I realised that it had always been there, I was just not aware of it and the effect it was having. I have become totally fascinated by it over the past two years and because I now know how it works, I have used it to my advantage and you can too!

The Law of Attraction, just like the Law of Gravity, has always been there and always will be. The universe is operating constantly to bring you the events and circumstances that appear in your life. I know this may sound a bit deep, but I strongly recommend that you get your head around this one because it can have a massive effect on your life.

I realised that because I had written out my goals and had pictures everywhere of the things I wanted to achieve, the Law of Attraction had been working to help me accomplish everthing on my list. When you write out your goals or put up pictures of them, you are constantly thinking about them, they are at the forefront of your mind.

You attract into your life the things you think about the most. This doesn't just apply to things that you want. If you think too much about what you don't want, you will attract that too! For example, if you are thinking 'I don't want to be shy', you will feel even more so. This is because it is your subconscious mind that is working here. Although you know what it is that you want and what it is that you don't want, the universe doesn't distinguish between want and don't want, it just recognises the thought and delivers it to you. So instead you should be thinking, 'I want to be confident'.

When you know about the Law of Attraction, and understand how it works, goal setting makes so much sense. If you are filling your mind with thoughts of the things you really want, there is no room for thought about the things you don't want. The mind cannot think about good things and bad things at the same time. Start to use the Law of Attraction to your advantage. Cut out thoughts of anything negative from your life and concentrate on the things that you want. When you are focussing on the positive things that you want, you cannot focus on negative things at the same time. Therefore you will start to attract only good things into your life.

## Gratitude

A great place to start if you want to make changes for the better and start attracting good things is to make a list of everthing you are grateful for. You may not be too overjoyed that you have been blessed with shyness, but what other qualities do you have that you really are grateful for? What else do you have in your life that you really appreciate? Do you have a loving family, children, a comfortable home, a car that gets you from A to B, a close friendship? We so often take things for granted. Start to really appreciate everything that you have in your life. If you are grateful for what you already have, you will get more of what you want.

It can be quite difficult to get into the habit of feeling grateful when you first start. However, I came across an idea that helped me to remember to be grateful throughout the day. I carry a gratitude rock, just a little pebble that fits neatly into my pocket. Every time I touch it I think of something that I am grateful for. Some days I only touch it when I put it into my pocket first thing in the morning and when I take it out last thing at night. But at least that is twice a day that I am feeling gratitude. Most days I touch it more that that. When you have been carrying your rock for some time, it becomes a habit to be grateful, so much so that you don't need the rock anymore.

*Get into the habit of gratitude!*

Gratitude is a great feeling to have. It shifts our energy into the right place for attracting good things.

## Be happy

Another way of making sure you are taking advantage of the Law of Attraction is to make sure that as much as possible you are in a happy state of mind. Do things that you love as much as you can. I know this can sometimes be difficult when you work and have other commitments but it is very important that you are happy.

Sometimes the simplest things can make us feel good. Just going for a walk or a drive and listening to some of your favourite music can put you into a happy state of mind. You could even take up a new hobby or sport. At the other end of the scale you could think about a career change if you are really unhappy in your job. Whatever it is that makes you happy, just try to find as much time on a weekly basis as you possibly can to immerse yourself into it.

One of my favourite words is *abundance*. I believe that we are all entitled to a life that is abundant in every way and we should not have to scrape through life managing with less than we would like. There is plenty of everything out there for everyone so I urge you to go out and get it!

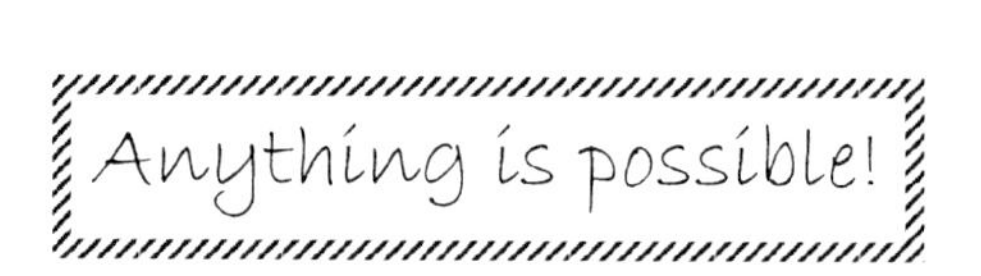


## Using affirmations

An affirmation is a positive statement about yourself or a statement about something that you want to achieve. Using positive affirmations has really helped me. You don't have to say them out loud, although it helps! Jaime and I have a lot of fun with affirmations, we say them together and laugh about it, but do you know something? It works!

If you write down your affirmations and put them somewhere where you will see them on a regular basis, you can then say them to yourself. This is better than not saying them at all.

Here are a few examples of affirmations, but you can use anything that you feel will help **you**:

*'I have more than enough time'*

*'I am a very successful person'*

*'I am a competent parent'*

*'I am confident and believe in myself'*

*'I believe that something amazing is going to happen to me today'*

## Expect the best

You get what you expect, so only expect the best. Throughout our lives our brains actually learn what to expect next, so it is really important that we only hold positive thoughts and expectations in our minds. Some people go through life expecting everything to go wrong, and guess what, it does! Why not expect everything to go right? Why not expect that you are going to act confidently and professionally whenever you need to? If you are going to expect things you might as well expect good things!

## Act as though you are already achieving

On the way to your goals, you should act like you have already achieved them. This means behaving like, talking like, dressing like, thinking like and feeling like the person who has achieved what you want to achieve.

Play the part. By doing this you are letting your subconscious mind know exactly what it is that you want so that it can then get to work on bringing those things to you.

## Take Action

If you want to achieve your goals and attract good things towards you, you must take positive action. Nothing happens without action. Break down the actions required to achieve your goal into bite size pieces and work through them one at a time. To help you do this, use the daily to do list and the weekly planner that I talk about in the next chapter. Reward yourself by achieving smaller goals along the way. You will gain a tremendous amount of satisfaction as you accomplish each individual task.

When you use the Law of Attraction, you will find that sometimes action will not feel like action because it is 'inspired' action. You are so passionate about the task in hand that you are totally immersed in it and it will feel effortless to you.

On the other hand, if you are constantly rushed off your feet, and feel permanenty stressed, you will not be in the right frame of mind to attract anything but more rush and stress! There is no point running yourself ragged to fit everything in. You will not accomplish half as much as you would if you would just take time out to look at how you could adjust a few things to make life run more smoothly. Carrying out your tasks in a relaxed, enjoyable way is far more effective and you will get much more done.

## Copy successful people

If you think back to when you were at school, you will remember how maybe you or others in your class were told off for copying. Sound familiar? What I have discovered, is that when you mix with successful people in your working life, it is quite the opposite!

If you ask any successful person how they got to where they are, they will be more than happy to tell you and to give you advice. If there is an area in which you would love to become successful, just find someone who has done it already and copy them. It's as easy as that. Offer to take them for lunch and spend a couple of hours finding out all you can.

## Spending time with the right people

You have to be careful who you spend your time with. Some people empower us, whereas some people seem to drain all our energy.

Now that you are starting out on the path to success, you need to make sure that you are in the presence of positive people as much as you can. Positive people will encourage you and support you.

Some people will try to knock you down and tell you that you will never achieve your dreams. We call them the 'dream stealers'. Try to stay away from these people and if you can't, at least take what they say with a pinch of salt!

Never lose sight of your dreams!

# Chapter 6 – Lets get organised

Just feeling that you are more in control and that you are organised goes a long way to improving your confidence and belief in yourself, therefore allowing you to pursue your dream life.

Getting organised needn't be complicated. Just by putting a few simple ideas into place, I managed to simplify my hectic life. Juggling children and running a business from home hasn't been easy but I have discovered ways to make it run more smoothly.

Planning your time can make a massive difference in your life whether you are a stay at home mum, director of your own company or both!

Now, first of all, for those of you who work from home, I personally feel that you cannot work at home at the same time as looking after young children. The two just do not go together. Don't get me wrong, working from home is great when you have kids because you can arrange your time so that you can be there to take them to and from school, be at sports days, concerts etc. when they are older. You can also work in the evenings when they are in bed, but when they are young and still at home with you, you can guarantee that as soon as you attempt to answer the telephone, or work on the computer you will be in demand, even if they seemed to be occupying themselves just perfectly a minute ago!

## Divide your time

One of the first things I did was to split the week into family time and work time. Once you have decided on when each is going to happen, stick to it. Promise yourself that you will not let one get in the way of the other. This shouldn't be too difficult if you work in a conventional job with set hours, but if you work for yourself, it is vital that you stick to your plan.

When it is family time it is 'family time' and this means either letting the answer phone take the calls or getting out of the house altogether, preferably without the mobile phone! If absolutely necessary, keep it with you just for emergencies. When it is work time it is 'work time' and this means that you have found suitable child care for your children somewhere that you are not! From past experience, I stress that if you work from home, you make sure your children are looked after elsewhere. Your work time will not be quality work time if you are constantly answering the office door to a crying child informing you of what the other child did to him or her. It also makes life very difficult for the person who is in charge of caring for the children.

So make life easier for everyone involved and make suitable arrangements so that you can carry out your work properly. Even if doing it this way may seem like you are not spending as much or enough time on your work, you will be surprised how much you get done in a smaller amount of time simply because you are not being interrupted or distracted.

> When it is work time, work!
> When it is play time, play!

## Daily 'to do' list

The second thing I was taught that helped me tremendously was to have a daily to do list. I didn't think this was necessary at first. I thought I could store everything in my head but I was amazed at how much more I got done when I started to use it.

All that you have to do is write out a list before you go to bed of all the things you have to do the next day. This way you are never starting the next day until it is completed on paper. As you go through your tasks throughout the day you will get great satisfaction as you tick things off one by one. When you get to the end of the day, if there are any tasks that you haven't crossed off your list, make sure that these tasks get carried over onto the list for the next day. It is also a good idea to complete the tasks that you are not looking forward to doing first, so that they are out of the way early on.

## Keep a diary

Thirdly a very simple one - keep a diary. Sounds obvious but I didn't have one until I started running the business. Now, I don't know how I coped without one! Write everything down in your diary whether it is work related, family related or social. You can keep two diaries one for each but personally I prefer to have just one with plenty of space for everything so that you don't miss anything. You don't want to find yourself in an important meeting when you should be collecting your daughter from a piano lesson! The best way is to keep one diary and fold each page in half and use one half for work and the other half for everything else.

## Weekly planner

Finally, similar to a diary, but something that I just use for business purposes, is a weekly planner. Again very simple it is just an A4 sheet of paper with the days of the week across the top and the hours of the day down the side.

The purpose of the weekly planner is to write down everything that needs to be done and at what time on what day you are going to do it. Before you fill in anything on your weekly planner you must block off all the time you cannot spend on your personal development or business due to other commitments. For example when I was running the business alongside my full time job, I blocked off all the time spent on my job including travelling time and when I had given up the job to have the children and run the business, I blocked off the time that was dedicated to looking after them. You can then realistically look at the time you have to play with to get everything done.

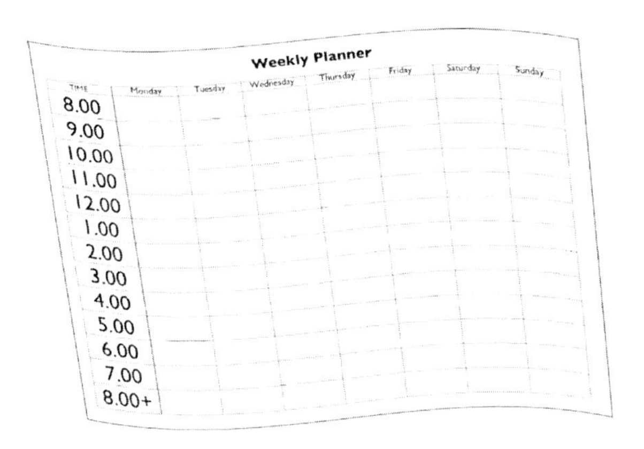


There are other little ways of getting more out of your day. For example, if you have children, when you have dropped them off at school it is very tempting to go straight home, but if you have things that you need to do that are out of the house, I suggest that you go and do them without returning home first. Make sure you have made time to have some breakfast before leaving the house or at least wrap some toast in foil and take it and a flask of coffee with you, anything to prevent you from sneaking back home, because once you have got comfy you will keep putting off leaving the house. The overflowing washing basket becomes unbearable to stare at any longer and before you know it you've loaded the washing machine, taken the dog for a walk, answered the phone, chatted to your neighbour who happened to knock on the door, unloaded the washing machine and put the clothes into the tumble dryer, all the things that would have had to have waited anyway if you had a conventional job to go to!

The business I work in involves a lot of outdoor activity and also a lot of appointments at various places so I always try to make my first appointment at a time that gives me just enough travelling time from school, and I have everything prepared and in the car before I leave in the morning.

If you think about it, popping back home even for half an hour each day can lose you two and a half hours a week of productive time.

## A few tips to end this chapter:

- At the end of every day when you think that you have done everything you can possibly do to move towards your dreams, do one more thing.

- An imperfect plan started today is better than a perfect plan started tomorrow. Just get started.

- It's not the hours you put in; it's what you put into the hours.

- Keep a notebook and pencil by your bed. You may get an idea during the night and chances are you won't remember it in the morning.

Without planning and time management, even the most confident and outgoing people cannot be successful.

Do you know that most people spend more time planning a holiday or a wedding than they do planning their lives? Scary but true!

# Chapter 7 - Give your children a great start!

This chapter is predominantly for those of you with children, but if you don't have children, please don't miss this one out because the information may be valuable in areas of your life too. You may have young people in your family or there maybe people who are infuenced by you.

I am extremely lucky that I had an amazing childhood and great parents to bring me up, I never really went short of anything. But, being an only child, I was very shy, kept myself to myself a lot and so never really developed any confidence.

Our children seem to have tons of confidence so I am not worried in any way that they will struggle with shyness like I did, but there are still many ways in which we can start helping them at this early age.

When you start to surround yourself with positive information and positive people and you are reading and working on yourself, it is also a great benefit to your children and the people around you. They will notice the difference in you, your positive attitude, and, it will make an impression on them too.

We have some friends who we have known for several years and when we met them, their two girls were very young. We have watched them grow up surrounded by personal development, always in positive company because their parents are continually learning and studying success. The two girls are now grown up and have moved out of the family home. They are two of the most level headed, confident and genuinely nice girls that you would ever wish to meet. One of them even started their own business at the age of 17 and is doing extremely well. She attends seminars and events with her parents and is continually developing herself.

Here are some things you can do to give children a fantastic start. Don't think that if you have or know older children that it is too late to start. It is **never** too late to start these good habits. Start from today!

## Encourage them to read

All sorts of books are a benefit to children, but as they become old enough to understand, you can introduce them to personal development. There are lots of books now aimed at children that teach them about wealth and success. They don't receive this sort of education at school so they will have a tremendous advantage if you can introduce them to it yourself. See the reading list at the end of the book.

## Teach them to save 10 percent

When children receive money for Christmas, birthdays or other occasions, teach them to put at least 10 percent of it into a money box. This will get them into the habit of saving from an early age.

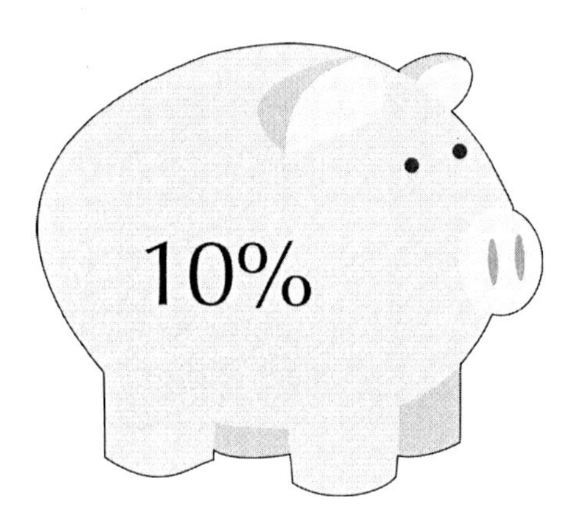


## Give them the opportunity to learn a language

Children are amazing at learning languages. They will learn as many new languages as you will teach them. They do not lack the capacity; they only ever lack the teachers. You can start by just introducing them to some of the many fabulous books that are out there. Our children learned their basic Spanish words from a few simple picture books.

## Show them how to dream

Make a dream board with them by cutting pictures out of magazines and catalogues and show them how to set goals. Children love to 'cut and stick'.

## Gratitude

Teach them how to be grateful. This may not be easy with children, however, use every opportunity you can to explain to them why they should appreciate what they have. Start by being grateful yourself. It's amazing how attitudes are contagious.

## The kiss in the pocket technique

I had to include this excellent idea which is a great technique to share with your children to enable them to feel confident and secure when they most need it.

I picked this up from one of my favourite mentors, Jan Ruhe. You can use it whenever you think your child may need a little bit of reassurance that you are not far away, for example, when they go to school for the first time or when they start a new school or go into a different class. It is so simple but so effective, you simply give them a kiss in their hand and tell them to hide it somewhere where no one else but they will know about it. The obvious ones are in a pocket or in a shoe, but there are lots of other places too. You explain to them that if they need to they can reach for their kiss throughout the day and then put it back safely until they need it again. They immediately feel special because they have something that no-one else has and they have the belief that everything is going to be ok.

These few simple ideas will certainly set your children off on the right track and give them an advantage as they are growing up.

# Conclusion - What do you do now?

The information that I have shared with you in this book is only going to be of benefit to you if you take action on it. I hope you feel inspired to go out and make a change in your life for the better.

I know that if you take on board just some of the ideas that I have covered, you will start to see a difference. You will begin to feel a lot more confident and successful and inevitably, you will start to lead a much happier life.

## Here is how you make a start, right now:

Begin your success journey by actioning at least the following:

- define what 'success' means to you
- write down your list of goals
- begin a reading routine
- do something you enjoy
- start practicing your communication skills

If you want to add anything else at this stage you can, if not the above are quite sufficient for the time being.

When you have written your 'action' list, put it somewhere where you will constantly notice it and have pleasure in ticking the tasks off the list as you accomplish them.

Congratulations, you have made a start. You are on the road to success!

Start to really believe in yourself. Don't let your shyness stand in your way. You are capable of achieving whatever it is that you want to achieve. You can be a success!

Get into the habit of being grateful for what you already have so that you are in the right mindset to receive further opportunities.

You might want to study some of the topics that are covered in this book in more detail. There are numerous books, audios and even DVDs available on each subject. Just visit your local library, bookstore or search the internet.

Finally, because I want to reach as many people as possible with this book, I would really like you to help me too. The ideas I have shared with you have helped me so much that I don't know where I would be now if I hadn't come across them. I feel so fortunate to have been in a position where I became exposed to the information. If you feel that this book has helped you, I urge you to pass on the information to people you know who may benefit from it too. Life is too short to hide away because you are shy. It is too short to be unhappy in what you do. Life is to be grabbed with both hands and enjoyed to the max!

I have proved that shy people can be successful too. (Remember by the way, that what success means to me may not necessarily be what it means to you.)

I now lead a lifestyle that a lot of people dream of and I can honestly say that it is down to the things that I have learned and practiced along the way. Although I now believe in myself and have a lot more confidence, I have not changed my personality in any way, and by no means am I an extrovert. I never will be, because that's not me.

If you have a genuine desire to improve your life, you **can**, and I wish you all the success in the world!

Remember:

Shy People Can Be Successful Too!

www.adeledecaso.com

# The power of music

What is it about certain song tracks? They seem to empower us, give us confidence, give us energy and make us feel absolutely great. Putting on one of your favourite song tracks is a great way of giving yourself a boost if you feel down. There are songs that just seem to have the feel good factor about them and there are others that when you here them they remind you of good times. Here is a list of some of my favourites. You may want to use some of these or put together a compilation of your own favourites.

The Winner Takes It All – Abba

Walking on Sunshine - Katrina & The Waves

One Moment In Time - Whitney Houston

Proud - Heather Small

You're a Superstar – Love Inc.

Lola's Theme - Shapeshifters

Blessed - Elton John

The Voice Within - Christina Aguilara

Hero - Mariah Carey

I'm Alive - Celine Dion

Julie Andrews - My Favourite Things

# My favourite books and audios

The Art of Exceptional Living – Jim Rohn (the first ever audio I listened to)

The One Minute Millionaire – Mark Victor Hanson and James Allen (my life changing read)

Read & Grow Rich – Burke Hedges

Feel the Fear & Do It Anyway – Susan Jeffers

Chicken Soup for the Soul Series – Jack Canfield & Mark Victor Hanson

7 Strategies for Wealth & Happiness – Jim Rohn

The Science of Getting Rich – Wallace D Wattles

Follow Your Heart – Andrew Matthews

Rich Dad, Poor Dad – Robert Kiyosaki

The One Minute Mother – Spencer Johnson

Excuse Me, Your Life is Waiting – Lynn Grabhorn

The Secret – Rhonda Burn

How to Get from Where You Are to Where You Want to Be – Jack Canfield

S.U.M.O (Shut Up, Move On) – Paul McGee

The Greatest Salesman in the World – Og Mandino

## Childrens' titles – although great for adults too!

Incredible You – Dr. Wayne Dyer

It's Not What You've Got – Dr. Wayne Dyer

Unstoppable Me –Dr. Wayne Dyer

Escape From The Rat Race - Robert Kiyosaki with Sharon L. Lechter

# My Goals

# My Goals

# My Goals

# Notes